Whodidit?

A Comedy

Neil Harrison

A Samuel French Acting Edition

FOUNDED 1830

SAMUELFRENCH-LONDON.CO.UK
SAMUELFRENCH.COM

FOR AMATEUR PRODUCTION ENQUIRIES

UNITED KINGDOM AND WORLD
EXCLUDING NORTH AMERICA
plays@SamuelFrench-London.co.uk
020 7255 4302/01

Each title is subject to availability from Samuel French,

depending upon country of performance.

WHODIDIT?

First performed at the Southside Community Centre, Edinburgh, on the 22nd July 1989 with the following cast:

Smart/Inspector	John MacIsaac
Mary/Shutters/Meals	Carrie McCarthy
Bonecrusher/Uncle/Travis/Shutters/Tom Jnr	Ian Cairns
Scribbles/Susan/Skakles	Carol McGowan
Darling/Stableman/Professor/Shutters	Nick Lawrence

Directed by Neil Harrison
Lighting and sound by Craigie Shiech

CHARACTERS

Laura **Scribbles**, totally illogical but likeable maid; early 20s

Mary Darling, the prissy, subservient wife of Tom Darling; 35ish

Able **Bonecrusher**, a madman

Constable **Smart**, the village policeman

Uncle, fiendishly bad-tempered, wheelchair-bound; octogenarian

Tom **Darling**, a dull, pipe-smoking, chauvinistic novelist; mid-30s

Detective **Inspector** Story, dashingly handsome, public-school-educated

Mrs **Meals**, an annoying cook; mid-50s

Young Danny **Travis**, breezy nephew of Tom and Mary; late teens

Stableman, Gentle John, gruff. Broad regional accent

Susan Daguerreotype, Tom's alcoholic sister; 35-ish

Jeanie **Skakles**, the crude gardener. Broad regional accent

Professor, Michael Headache, the old, invisible, violent professor

Tom Darling **Jnr.**, the annoying son of the Darlings; 10

Shutters, a very strange butler

The action of the play takes place on an empty stage

Time — the 1920s

AUTHOR'S NOTES

COSTUME

As parts are doubled in this play, the costumes should be simple, to allow for quick changes. The following costumes and identifying props are possibilities:

Laura Scribbles A twenties-style sensible pinafore-type uniform and a period duster

Mary Darling A slightly dull period sensible dress

Able Bonecrusher A showy but smart period suit

Constable Smart A period police overcoat, helmet and truncheon. He has huge black whiskers

Uncle He sits in a period wheelchair with a blanket over his legs. His top half is dressed as a big game hunter; he wears a skirt under the blanket. He wears glasses and has a moustache

Tom Darling A brown period suit with a cravat. He smokes a pipe

Inspector A plain-clothes officer in a period trenchcoat. He smokes a pipe

Mrs Meals An apron which has been stuffed to give a heavy appearance, a cook's hat and wooden spoon

'Young' Danny Travis A pin-striped jacket, white trousers and boater

Gentle John Wellingtons, flat cap and a white shirt with rolled-up sleeves

Susan Daguerreotype An idiosyncratic period dress. She carries a gin bottle

Jeanie Skakles A long gardening coat and a hat decorated with withered flowers

Tom Darling Jnr. Short trousers, white shirt and school cap

Shutters A sober butler's suit, but a ridiculous wig

The personal props listed here are real; other props are mimed (See *Furniture and Property List* p.45)

DOUBLING

Whodidit? can be performed by cast as small as five or by a large cast of up to seventeen. When the play is performed by a small cast, not only do the actors take multiple roles, but the role of the butler, Shutters, is split between three actors. It would work as follows:

Shutters' first appearance is made by the actor playing Mary, his second by the actor playing Darling, the third by the actor playing Bonecrusher, the fourth again by the actor playing Darling.

In all performances, the role of Shutters will have greatest effect when split between three actors.

Neil Harrison

WHODIDIT?

This play is performed with absolutely no set. The various settings are brought to life through lighting, sound effects and mime

When the play begins, the set is, nominally, a period drawing-room with a fireplace, phonogram, chairs etc. (All imaginary.)The room is in darkness. Music is playing. A doorbell rings

The Lights gradually come up to reveal Mary Darling "opening the curtains" DC, facing the audience. The music fades. The door bell rings again

Mary Laura! Answer the door, you silly girl — and send the caller into this spacious period drawing-room. (*Pause*) And tidy that hair!

Mary mimes opening more curtains whilst humming the music played at the beginning of the play. She moves to the phonogram, lifts the record from it and flips it over to look at the reverse side

Able Bonecrusher enters and stands in the doorway

Bonecrusher Mary Darling?
Mary Yes?
Bonecrusher I'm an exceedingly handsome chap from *Modern Home* magazine. I was immediately attracted by this *magnificent* mansion on the hill — and would dearly love to feature it in our September issue.
Mary Oh, how simply marvellous! Do come in, Mr, ah …
Bonecrusher (*walking towards Mary*) Bonecrusher. (*He kisses her*

hand) Able Bonecrusher. This *is* an attractive room! So nice to see a house with good crackling fireplace.

The sound effect of a loud blast of crackling fire, snapping quickly on and off, is heard

But I'm *especially* charmed by the Queen Anne upright chairs. (*He makes to sit down*) May I sit down?

Mary quickly dives over to stop Bonecrusher from falling over (because, of course, there is no chair)

Mary No! Ah, they've just been varnished.

Mary provides the next sound effect — that of a dog barking. She is oblivious to Bingo's fate during the following and smiles throughout

Bonecrusher (*greeting the imaginary dog*) Hallo! (*He pats the dog*)
Mary That's Bingo! (*She makes the noises of the dog barking and panting*) He's a dinky little darling, don't you think?
Bonecrusher (*still patting*) I like him. I like him very much. (*He picks the dog up; in a changed tone*) *I* had a puppy once. I liked *him*. I liked him a *lot*. I liked to hug him. People say I don't know my own strength, Mrs Darling. (*He becomes very strange*) I hugged him and hugged him and hugged him and after that he didn't seem to want to go for walks.

The dog yelps, more and more as the speech goes on

He didn't want to eat and he didn't want to lick my face. He just slept and slept and slept. He slept for two whole years.

Bingo lets out a final yelp

Do you think he was tired from all the hugging? (*He releases Bingo, who falls to the floor*)

There is a thud — provided off-stage

Mary (*still oblivious: still smiling*) I expect he was, Mr Bonecrusher.

The sound of the falling dog has taken Bonecrusher out of his mad turn. He is surprised to find the dead dog at his feet. He picks it up, looks to the fire, and tosses the dog into it

I'm sure your readers will be interested in the sophisticated french windows ——

There is the sound of Bingo in the fire; a loud burst of crackling fire

— they're all the rage this season, I'm told.

Mary opens the imaginary windows. We hear gentle birdsong, followed by noisy seagulls, followed by loud tropical squawks; the sequence perhaps ends with an elephant trumpeting

The doorbell rings. This is quickly followed by a lightning flash

Excuse me, Mr Bonecrusher. (*Calling*) Laura! The door! (*To Bonecrusher*) She's such a scatterbrained child. I really should ——

Bonecrusher claps his hand over Mary's mouth

— UGG! ——
Bonecrusher (*severely*) I'll handle this! Just keep your bloody damned blasted mouth shut!

There is a roar of thunder and a simultaneous lightning flash

Constable Smart enters

Smart Ay, that storm's fair ragin' out there.

Smart shakes hands with Bonecrusher and Mary; the latter is still being silenced

Afternoon. Sorry to bother you, Mr and Mrs Darling, but I'm afraid there's been a bit of trouble at the village and we're looking for an escaped crazy nut-case. A mad psycho on the run. Ken what I mean? A *right* bloody comedian. Anyway, you havenae seen anything strange this afternoon have ye, sir?

Bonecrusher (*polite but formal*) No. Everything here has been lovely.

Smart And you, missus?

Bonecrusher She's seen nothing.

Smart Can the lassie no speak for hersel', sir?

Bonecrusher No — my hands are over her mouth.

Smart Right ye are. (*Cheery*) Well, if either of you do see anything of a suspicious nature, then do not hesitate to contact me at my rather quaint police station. The number's Farmbright 206. Just ask for PC Smart. Cheers!

Smart exits, singing a current advertising jingle

Bonecrusher and Mary remain still for a moment

Bonecrusher Now, I'm going to release my grip. If you should scream … (*He releases his grip on Mary*)

Mary Now, as I was saying, I really *should* replace that silly girl, Laura. She is *impossible*!

Bonecrusher (*charmingly*) She's feeble-minded, but charming all the same.

The doorbell rings

(*Severely*) Who will *that* be?

Mary My darling husband, Tom. I do so love him!

Bonecrusher (*dragging Mary towards an exit*) One squeak out of you and you'll jolly well never see him again!

Bonecrusher exits, pulling Mary with him

Tom Darling enters from the opposite side of the stage, smoking a real pipe

Darling Hallo! Anyone home? Hall-oa! It's me, Tom Darling: tall, handsome, pipe-smoking novelist husband of the charmingly pretty Mary Darling! Hall-oa!

Uncle enters from the opposite side of the stage to Darling. He is in a real wheelchair with a real rug across his knees

Uncle Oh, hallo, Tom. Nice afternoon?

Darling Tiring, Uncle. Tiring. Yourself?

Uncle Very pleasant, old boy. I've been stuffing an elephant's head all day.

Darling Good for you, Uncle!

Uncle Shot the old boy in Africa forty years ago. Left the blasted thing in my bedroom. Forgotten all about the silly damned blighter till today. He'll look bloody good in your bedroom; what do you think, Tom? Next to the rhino I gave you last year.

Darling I'll—ah—think it over, Uncle. (*Pause*) Is my darling wife Mary around?

There is a violent scream from Mary, off. Pause

Uncle Haven't heard so much as a squeak out of her all day, old boy.

Mary enters at speed, distressed

Mary Oh, Tom, darling! Thank *God* you're back! (*She bursts into tears*)

Darling (*cheery*) For goodness sake, darling! What's all the fuss? I've only been *gone* a few hours!

Mary There's a beastly man upstairs and he's trying to kill me!

Darling *Non*sense, darling.

Uncle Fiddlesticks, Mary!

Mary He says he's going to kill us all! (*She buries her head in Tom's chest*)

Darling (*affectionately*) Darling. What a frightful imagination you have! (*He catches Uncle's eye and smiles*) Maybe you should be the writer!

Darling and Uncle laugh loudly, starting and stopping simultaneously

Mary But I'm not imagining things! He's up there now. Oh, Tom, he's going to kill me! (*She bursts into tears*)

Darling and Uncle laugh again, as above

He *is*, Tom! He *is*!
Darling (*annoyingly playful*) Oh, he *is*, is he?
Uncle Bosh!
Darling Uncle's right. It's sheer nonsense. You're just tired, darling. You've been overdoing things — playing the phonogram and taking strenuous afternoon naps.
Mary But the man said he was ——
Uncle Twaddle!
Mary But *listen* to me ——
Darling (*cutting Mary off*) Ah, ah! (*Calmly and reassuringly*) Whoever it was, they've gone now. Everything is fine. *I'm* here.

Pause

Mary Are you sure, Tom?
Darling Of *course* I'm sure! I'm your husband, aren't I? Just don't you worry your pretty little head about it.
Mary Oh, I'm sorry to be such a silly girl, Tom.
Darling That's quite all right, Mary. You've *always* been silly. I'm *glad* you're silly. I wouldn't have *married* you if you *weren't* silly. (*Pause*) Now, how about nipping upstairs and fetching my slippers, silly girl?
Mary (*sniffing*) Of course, Tom. (*She heads for the exit*) Have you had a hard day, darling?
Darling (*filling his pipe*) Rather! The blasted publishers have been asking my advice on the blinking typeface of my new novel, "Murder is Illegal".
Uncle Disgraceful!
Mary Oh, you poor, poor thing!

Mary exits

Uncle *Nasty* business, Tom. *Nasty* business.
Darling Yes, typography *does* strain one's nerves.
Uncle A *damnable* nuisance, Tom!
Darling Yes.
Uncle Downright *filthy* if you ask me, you poor devil!
Darling Quite.

Pause

Uncle Stinking bad luck, you old bugger!
Darling Steady on, old boy — it's not *that* bad!
Uncle (*wheeling himself towards the exit*) Of course it is, Tom — it's bloody horrific! Anyway, I thought your new novel was entitled "Stabbed by a Gun"?
Darling No, Uncle — that was the one I wrote *last* week.
Uncle I see.

Uncle exits

Mary screams, off

Darling (*merely curious*) Hallo?

Mary runs screaming into the room. Bonecrusher strolls on after her, grinning

Mary Oh, Tom, Tom — it's him!

Darling and Bonecrusher greet each other with a friendly, hearty laugh

Darling Able! It's been years!
Bonecrusher (*charmingly*) But you haven't changed one bit, Tom!
Mary That's him, Tom. The wicked man! That's him!
Darling Nice to see you — wicked man!

Bonecrusher Likewise, old sport!

Mary (*in disbelief*) You *know* the fiend, Tom?

Darling Know him! We were best friends at university! Able Bonecrusher — practical joker *extraordinaire*! For the first two years we never understood a *word* old Able here said — he pretended he was Dutch! (*Pause*) But he wasn't! (*He laughs*) Oh, *how* we all laughed! I'll never forget the time you hid inside a desk for a year and then *sprang* out, just when everyone thought you were dead! Oh, how we all laughed!

Mary Sounds like an damned *im*practical joker if you ask me, Tom.

Bonecrusher (*kissing Mary's hand*) I'm not mad, Mrs Darling — just amusing.

There are dramatic chords and thunder, with a flash of lightning just after the third chord

The Inspector enters. The audience does not see his face. Everyone on stage gasps

Inspector (*holding out his hand*) Please! Do not be disturbed by my looks.

They all scream hysterically

I may *look* like a monster, but I assure you that, underneath, I am the same as you or I. I'm Detective Inspector Harry Story of Scotland Yard. My car's stuck in a ditch half a mile down the road. I came for the use of your telephone. Sorry if I startled you.

Darling Good heavens, man! You must be the ugliest fellow that ever lived!

The Inspector turns to the audience; he is actually quite dashing

Inspector (*calmly*) No, there was a man living in Cornwall in the late thirteenth century. Now, I don't know how far you can go on rumour and hearsay, but, apparently this man was so damned ugly that the only employment he could get was as a scarecrow. A damned ugly scarecrow, by all accounts. Trouble was he was too damned ugly. And he didn't just scare crows. He frightened every species of bird in a ten-mile radius and so the insect population multiplied like nobody's business. Soon the whole eco-system became imbalanced and the bug-infested crops were totally destroyed. (*Pause*) The villagers weren't easy on the poor blighter. (*He shakes his head*) They sawed off his head and hosted the biggest damned inter-village five-a-side football tournament the county had ever seen. (Some bloody good goals, by all accounts.) They buried his body in the local churchyard — no problem on that score. But his head was destined for an altogether less holy resting place. They dug a hole a mile deep in the village green, into which they tossed this poor blighter's noggin. And for ten years, every man, woman and child urinated on it three times a day. I hope that you can treat me in a more civilized fashion — after all, it's not the Middle Ages, is it?

Darling But your bloody face, man!

Bonecrusher You almost frightened the life out of us!

Mary (*pointing at the Inspector*) How *dare* you bring that — that — *thing* this close to decent law-abiding people!

Darling Able, *please* — take my wife for a stroll. His face may interfere with her unborn children.

Mary (*shielding her line of vision*) I'll show you the family jewels, Mr Bonecrusher.

Bonecrusher I'd like that very much!

Mary and Bonecrusher exit

Darling (*severely*) Bloody hell, man. What the *deuce* did you do to deserve a face like that?

The Inspector hangs his head

I've seen more attractive men in Scotland! (*Still very severe*) There's a joke going round the taverns just now — something about teaching one's arse to speak. Know it, do you?

Inspector My gross disfigurement doesn't interfere with my ability to carry out my duties as a police officer, and that is what brought me to the village of Farmbright today: someone, possibly still in the village, has killed a large number of people in an unspeakably brutal fashion.

Thunderclap

Uncle enters

Uncle How many people has this diabolical fellow killed, might I ask?

Inspector We don't know for sure. Could be five — could be six. Could be a dozen. Could be a baker's dozen. He could have killed a dozen bakers — we *just don't know*!

Darling Such strange happenings, Inspector.

Inspector Yes. (*Pause*) Mr Darling, have you ever heard the name "Dracula"?

Darling (*uncertainly*) Drocula?

Inspector Dracula. *Count* Dracula.

Darling (*impatiently*) It seems a very silly name to me. No, I can't say I have, why?

Inspector You surprise me! Hollywood has made over two thousand films using him as the main character, but the gist of it was that *he,* Count Dracula, would suck the blood of his victims.

Darling Are you suggesting that this Count Drocula thing is killing people from the village?

Inspector I am merely suggesting, Mr Darling, that we're dealing with a similar evil.

Uncle Why, that's just a lot of — mumbo-jumbo! Belongs between the pages of Tom's harum-scarum novels! Pah! It's just gibbering jungle-talk! Hocus-pocus! Voodoo! Blatant tomfoolery! Far-fetched fiddle-faddle! Fudge! Bosh! Balderdash! Tommy rot!

Darling (*cutting in*) OK, Uncle, calm down.

Uncle All this talk about goblins and fairies!

Darling No-one said anything about goblins and fairies, Uncle!

Uncle Spooks and spirits!

Darling Uncle!

Uncle Demons and devils!

Darling Uncle, have a slug of meths, and shut up.

Uncle Fiddlesti ... oh, good idea, Tom! (*He produces a real bottle and drinks from it*)

There is an explosion off stage

Inspector What in the name of blazes —— !

Darling Oh, that's just Michael Headache, the mad professor.

Inspector You have a mad professor living here? Mmm. Can I see him?

Darling No, you can't. No-one can see him. Fifteen years ago, after a lifetime's research, he finally managed to make himself invisible. He's now working on phase two of the experiment.

Inspector Hence the explosion.

Uncle But he's harmless, Inspector. Not like our killer, who must be caught and hanged by the neck. (*He takes his glasses off*) And I must get my glasses seen to. (*He cleans his glasses*) Through these you look like a squealing hog caught in a trap, and *that* can't be right can it? (*He puts his glasses back on. There is a long pause as he takes a closer look at the Inspector*)

Uncle exits quickly, holding back sickness

There is a flash of lightning

Darling Terrible business. Me? I'm the cheery type — never dwelling on the morbid, but it'll get to the stage where no-one in the village will want to go out, for fear that they too will be crushed to a pulp.

Inspector (*slowly*) I didn't say how they had been killed, Mr Darling.

Darling (*edgily*) Oh, really? Well, I must have read it in the paper.

Inspector It won't appear until the late edition, sir.

Darling Well, I hope you can catch him quicker than they can report it! (*He gives a weak laugh. Pause. He is serious again*) As long as he is on the loose, not a person in the village will be safe.

Inspector The fact that each victim has been a person has been a closely guarded secret, Mr Darling.

Darling Oh? I just — assumed. (*Pause*) But, I don't understand! What kind of man would want to *do* that sort of thing? Leaving a childish rhyme on the body of each victim seems — to me at least — a *very* strange and curious thing to do!

Inspector Again, I never said that this particular practice was performed, sir.

Darling *Again*, I just *assumed*.

Inspector (*firmly*) You assume a *lot* of things, Darling!

Darling (*slightly camply*) No need to get stroppy, honey!

Mrs Meals enters to a thunder crack and simultaneous lightning

Meals Oh my! Oh my! It's Billy Gruff, the 'andy-man. 'E's dead, 'e is. 'E's dead! Oh my, oh my! It was 'orrible, it was. 'Orrible!

Darling Nasty business! Nasty business! Now, hurry up and finish making the blasted dinner! What do you think I pay you for! Being fat?

Meals I found him in the pantry — beaten to a pulp. 'Ardly recognizable, he was.

Inspector (*slowly, accusingly*) How *did* you recognize him then, cook?

Meals Oh, he *always* looked like a pulp. Very slovenly of face, 'e was — a bit like yourself, sir. Terrible business. Me? I'm the cheery type — always laughing, I am. (*She laughs hideously for a second*) I found this note on his body, sir. (*She hands the Inspector a real note*)

Inspector Mmm, it's in the form of a simple child's rhyme:
(*Reading*) "Not last night, but the night before,
      Three little monkeys came to the door,
      And crushed me to a pulp."
Mmmm, interesting metre. (*Suddenly loudly*) *You* did it, cook. You always hated him, *didn't* you? Hated him with every *bone* in your *body*! You couldn't stand it any longer. You *grabbed* him and he *screamed*! You told him to be quiet but he kept on screaming so you *hit* him but he wouldn't stop so you hit him

again! Something took you over. Something you don't understand. You saw yourself doing it but you didn't believe it was you! You felt *dizzy* and *strange* and he kept *on* screaming and you hit him *again* and *again* and *again* and you didn't mean to but you *killed* him, cook! You lost your mind and you killed him with your *bare hands*!

Meals I did not, sir!

Inspector Oh well, it's always worth a try. (*He takes out a real pad*) What was this chap's name, did you say?

Meals Billy Gruff, sir.

Inspector (*writing*) Billy Gruff. Did he have a middle name?

Scribbles enters at speed and curtsies

Scribbles Goats, beggin' your pardon, sir. Billy Goats Gruff.

Inspector (*surprised*) Hallo! And what's your name, you rather dotty gal?

Scribbles Laura Scribbles, sir, beggin' your pardon.

Inspector (*writing*) Scribbles. (*He looks at what he's written*) That's odd — I can hardly read that. (*To Meals*) And your name, cook?

Meals Me, sir? Mrs Meals, sir.

Inspector (*writing*) Well, Mrs Meals, tell me, did you see anything strange this afternoon?

Meals (*invading the Inspector's space*) No, sir, I keeps myself to myself, I do.

Inspector Very kind of you, I'm sure. Now, how about you, Laura? Did *you* hear anything ——

Meals Would sir like to eat a large selection of cakes?

There is a pause, during which the Inspector looks at Meals

Inspector (*harshly*) Go away, Mrs Meals.

Meals As you wish, sir.

Meals exits

Inspector As I was saying: Laura — did you hear anything funny this afternoon?

Scribbles No, sir—I were listening to Tommy Trinder on the radio, sir.

Inspector So, you didn't hear any shouts, screams, calls?

Pause

Scribbles Could you run that list by me again, beggin' your pardon, sir?

Inspector (*giving Scribbles a puzzled look. Uncertainly*) Why, certainly, Laura. (*Slowly and carefully*) Shouts? (*Pause*) Screams? (*Pause*) Calls?

Scribbles thinks for a minute

Scribbles One more time, if you don't mind, sir.

Inspector (*giving Scribbles a puzzled look. Uncertainly*) If you wish, Laura. Shouts? (*Pause*) Screams? (*Pause*) Ca — (*Aside*) I'm just wasting my time here, aren't I? (*To Laura*) Fetch me, Mrs Darling. I wish to ask *her* a few questions. And do something about that hair!

Scribbles Yes, sir.

Darling (*holding up his hand and stopping Laura*) Sir, my wife is a very delicate and feminine woman. It is not a ladylike thing to be discussing such morbid subjects. Besides, she's showing my friend the family jewels.

Inspector She's taking her time.

Darling She was born feet first, and tends to do things very slowly. A heartless but nevertheless true statement of fact.

Scribbles It's true, sir; no Albert Einstein was she, beggin' your pardon, sir.

Darling Laura, you will speak *only* when you are spoken to! Is that clear?

Scribbles Is what clear, sir?

Darling Just *stop insulting* my *wife*, Laura!

Scribbles Sorry, sir.

Pause

Darling And what do you mean "No Albert Einstein *was* she"?
Scribbles (*handing a real note to Darling*) Oh, this note was found on her body, beggin' your pardon, sir.

There is a Black-out with a simultaneous thunderclap. Music

The Lights come back up and the music fades

Darling has his head in his hands

Inspector So, you served her tea — and *then* what?
Scribbles I left and then curtsied, sir.
Inspector (*after a pause*) Shouldn't you — (*he curtsies*) — curtsy first, then leave?
Scribbles I didn't never have any complaints from Mrs Darling when *she* was alive, sir.
Darling This is irrelevant, Inspector!
Inspector Please, bear with me, Mr Darling. (*Pause*) Tell me, Laura, did you notice anything unusual about Mrs Darling whilst you were in the room?
Scribbles I don't recall, sir.
Darling Think, girl, think!
Scribbles Well, now that I come to think of it ——
Darling Come on, try and remember!
Scribbles Well, she did seem to be ——
Darling TRY AND REMEMBER!
Scribbles She looked like she was ——
Darling THINK, damn you, THINK!
Scribbles You're not giving me a chance!
Darling (*hysterically*) SHE'S HYSTERICAL!

Pause

Inspector Can you leave this to me please, Mr Darling? (*He puts Darling's pipe in Darling's mouth*) Go and have a few puffs of your pipe, there's a good chap. (*He pats Darling's back and turns to Laura*) Now, Laura, you were saying?

Scribbles Well, now that I comes to think of it, there *was* something odd.

Inspector Yes?

Scribbles A vicious madman had his evil hands round her delicate neck, begging your pardon, sir.

Darling (*covering his face with his hands*) My God! (*He walks away*) My God! My God! My God!

Scribbles Pardon me, sir — you never reacted like this when Ken Dodd's dad's dog died!

Darling turns to Laura

Darling (*after a pause; in disbelief*) Laura, I never gave two *hoots* for Ken Dodd's dad's dog!

Inspector And what's wrong with Ken Dodd's dad's dog, Darling? It always seemed a decidedly decent dog to *this* detective!

Darling Will you both shut up about Ken Dodd's dad's dog!! I'm *glad* the damned dalmatian's dead!

Inspector (*smiling*) Oh, come on, Mr Darling! You're just in a bad mood! When you look back on this in a few years time you too will see the — *funny* side of it all!

Darling (*distressed*) Can you not just concentrate on your job, Inspector?

Inspector Stay cool, Mr Darling. Hang loose. (*To Laura*) Now, Laura, could you describe this man for me? Was he broad?

Scribbles Broad, sir?

Inspector (*smiling mischievously*) Yes, did he have — large pectorals?

Scribbles Oh, I don't know, sir — he kept his trousers on all the time *I* was there.

Darling Inspector! My wife has just been murdered and you are playing the role of straight-man to a third-rate music hall comic!

Inspector (*holding up his hand*) My sincere apologies, Mr Darling. It *was* — *thoughtless* of me.

Darling Quite.

Inspector (*to the audience*) Now, let me think — should I risk this one? Why not! (*To Laura*) Now, the front door was locked, wasn't it? So he couldn't have got in *that* way, could he, Laura?

Scribbles No, sir — he must have been a back-door man.
Darling *Right,* Inspector! That's *it!* — *no* more questions! Laura, fetch me some blasted brandy from the cellar, you stupid girl!
Scribbles Yes, sir.

Scribbles exits

Inspector (*calling*) Is that wise? (*To Darling*) The murderer could be lurking down there. I heard some strange noises from below.
Darling Oh, that'll just be the sound of Shutters banging.
Inspector But I'm sure I heard voices. Sounded like a man and a woman.
Darling Yes, that's what I'm saying. It'll be Shutters and his girlfriend. It's the butler's day off.

Shutters enters

Oh, here he is now, coincidentally. Hallo, Shutters. Enjoying your day off?
Shutters Yes, thank you, sir.
Inspector You're very sinister-looking, Shutters.
Shutters I'm sorry, sir. I suppose you could say I'm a bit of a square-shouldered rough diamond. I heard the bad news. My grave condolences, sir. I suppose I'm a suspect?
Inspector (*taking out his notebook*) Everyone is. (*He looks Shutters up and down*) Shutters, can I take down your particulars?
Darling Inspector!
Inspector (*surprised*) Look, I didn't *mean* that one!
Shutters (*listing items*) My name is Shutters. I speak slowly with only the slightest hint of a foreign accent —— (*His tone suggests he is going to continue the list*)
Inspector And?
Shutters That's it, sir. That sums me up completely.
Inspector Fair enough. (*He smiles*) Shutters, could you give me a brief account of your — *movements* this afternoon?
Shutters A sort of rhythmical up and down, sir.
Darling Inspector! You're *feeding* these people these lines!

Sad violin music plays

Inspector (*suddenly upset*) Mr Darling, I have a very sad life. The only woman that ever kissed me was my mother. So please don't deny me the small pleasure that innuendo affords me. (*He becomes choked up*) It's the only thing that brings me comfort. (*He bursts into tears*)
Darling (*emotionally*) Why, man — I'm sorry. (*He holds back tears*) I didn't realize ——
Inspector It's all right — you weren't to know. (*He suddenly returns to normal*)

The music cuts out

I'm OK now. I hope your attic is sizeable. I fear that before dawn returns with her comforting light, there will be many more murders in this nightmarish mansion.

Thunder

Darling Nightmarish mansion? Don't get carried away, Inspector. You've been reading too many tatty little thrillers. (*He indicates the room*) On the contrary, this is a charming and elegant home. Why, I myself chose all the furnishings and *objets d'art* for their — their unpretentious lightness. Ikea.
Inspector (*pointing at an imaginary ornament*) What's that?
Darling (*proudly*) Oh, it's, just a conversation piece.
Inspector I see ...

They all look at the designated ornament. No-one speaks. They all stand around embarrassed, not able to think of anything to say. They begin to shuffle and cough. Sentences are almost begun, but ... The atmosphere and social discomfort become excruciating. The Inspector pulls out a real handkerchief and mops his brow. Darling borrows the handkerchief to mop his own brow. Shutters, oblivious, picks up the ornament and brings it closer to the others, holding a fixed smile

It's all too much for Darling, who exits on his tiptoes

Pause

Inspector Oh, put the bloody thing down, Shutters, will you!

Travis enters

Travis (*with extreme boyish enthusiasm*) Hallo, I'm Tom's nephew, Young Danny Travis! I'm a charming rather vague man in my late-teens-stroke-early-twenties. I've come to stay the weekend! Golly! What a super house! I'm especially charmed by the crystal chandelier. Yes, all-in-all, a charming and comfortable room. Pity about the ugly beggar by the fireplace.

Inspector You've arrived at a rather unfortunate time, Mr Young Danny Travis. Mr Darling's wife has just been murdered.

Travis Gosh, yes! Terrible business! Me? I'm the cheery type, always beating out a rhythm on my thighs. (*He beats out a frantic rhythm on his thighs during the following*) Go, man, go!

Inspector (*trying to stop Danny*) OK, young Danny, OK.

Danny (*continuing to drum*) Yeah! Yeah!

Inspector DANNY!

Danny Take me home, daddy!

Inspector *DANNY!*

Travis (*stopping and looking up*) Yes? Any requests?

Inspector (*firmly*) Do you know who killed Mrs Darling?

Travis I don't think so, but you hum it and I'll join in.

There is a burst of over-enthusiastic canned laughter and applause. Travis revels in it, bowing and thanking the audience. The Inspector grabs him by the collar. The audience laughter and applause cut out

Inspector Think you're smart, Sonny Jim? Now listen here! Did *you*, young Danny Travis, see anyone suspicious *in* or *near* the grounds as you came in?

Travis Why, yes — I did! I watched a strange chap saunter/stride out of the stables.

Inspector How would you describe him?
Travis Badly, I should think — I failed my standard grade English.
Inspector The stables eh? Shutters, take me to the stableman.

Travis, the Inspector and Shutters exit

Black-out

Two real pitchforks are set

Two seconds later the lights come up L

We are now — nominally — in a stable

> *The Stableman, Gentle John, leads an imaginary horse on and
> pats it. He then sets to work pitching hay*

The Inspector enters

Inspector Good-morning.
Stableman Morning? I've been up twelve hours — nearly time for
supper!
Inspector My, these grounds are exceptionally beautiful: a charming
old well, and stables made from ancient timbers. This place
carries an enormous charm.

Pause

Stableman Are you gay, Inspector? Because poetic musing don't
feed the horses. (*He pitches more*) This is honest hard work —
something you city folks wouldn't understand.
Inspector (*picking up a pitchfork*) Well, I may not be of the country,
but it doesn't mean I don't appreciate the feel of a good sturdy
implement in my hands.

There is a pause. The Stableman looks at the audience

Stableman You remind me of the officer who sent my comrades
to certain death — while he watched and smoked his pipe.

Inspector (*pitching*) Calm down, old boy.

Stableman Us men did the fighting. You people sat back and watched. Lambs to the slaughter.

Inspector And there's been a fair bit of that in Farmbright of late. You're out here in the fresh air all day. You must see a lot.

Stableman I see horses, Inspector. Horses 'n' hay. That's all.

Inspector Of course, only a man with strong hands could have crushed those people. I see you have strong and calloused hands, Mr Horseman.

Stableman (*seething*) I've got strong and gentle hands, Inspector. They calls me Gentle John round 'ere. Put your back into it, man!

Inspector Gentle? I detect a lot of pent-up violence.

Stableman I don't like your tone, Mr Detective.

Inspector I suppose a brutal man like you enjoyed the war, what with all the killing and such.

The two pitchforks clash

Stableman Just what are you trying to suggest, Inspector?

Inspector That you can't shake the demons of war. You're my number one suspect, Sonny Jim. And now I'm off to question suspect number two — the other brutal person of the household.

Stableman Mrs Meals, the cook?

Bonecrusher enters

Inspector The one and only.

The Inspector heads for the exit, bumping into Bonecrusher

The Inspector exits

Bonecrusher (*patting the horses in a strange way*) I like horses.

A horse neighs

I like them a lot.

A horse neighs

I had a horse once.

Stableman If you want to help, you can crush up some of those
rough oats for the young foal. She's a bit on the poorly side this
mornin'.

Bonecrusher looks at his hands

You'll have to use a mortice, though. The oats are down there.

Bonecrusher walks towards the Stableman with his arms outstretched

No, Mr Bonecrusher — I said down there! Mr Bonecrusher! NO!
NO! (*He screams*)

*The Lights cross-fade from L to R; as they do so, the scream gives
way to the sound of a whistling kettle*

The Stableman and Bonecrusher exit; the Inspector enters R

We are in a kitchen

*Meals enters, runs to the imaginary stove, switches off the gas and
lifts the kettle*

Meals Some tea, Inspector?

The sound of the whistle fades

Inspector Why, that would be lovely, Mrs Meals.

*During the next sequence, Mrs Meals mimes — very badly — a
variety of kitchen tasks*

Meals I don't mind telling you, Inspector, my nerves are in a right
  sorry state. It's been quite a day, it has!
Inspector Yes, you can say that again.

Meals makes to repeat herself

But — for the sake of your comic credibility, I wouldn't advise it.
Meals Such terrible goings on! Only a *scoundrel* could be killing
  those poor souls!
Inspector How would you describe *yourself*, Mrs Meals?
Meals I'm a cheery but practical woman with a large, ruddy face.
  And for your information, I couldn't hurt a fly. And if you want
  my advice, I'd look to Tom's black sheep of a sister — always
  stealing my sherry, that one is.
Inspector And does that make her capable of murder, Mrs Meals?
Meals I do believe it does, Inspector. It's the devil's juice, an' make
  no mistake. Now, can you pass me that extremely large cookbook
  down from the shelf, Ugly? I can't remember if it's *one or two*
  spoonfuls of yeast extract. (*She continues to mime and hum
  during the following*)

*The Inspector takes an unbelievably huge imaginary cookbook
down from a shelf*

Inspector (*struggling with the book*) It'll take you bloody ages to
  find — it's such a large blinking book!

*Meals takes the book; in her hands it turns into a pocket book. She
fixes the Inspector with a look in the eye, opens the book, randomly
plants her finger in it and looks to where the finger has landed*

Meals Ah, two spoonfuls. (*She hands the book back*) Will that be
  all, Inspector?
Inspector (*putting the "huge" book back. Sternly*) It certainly will
  not, Missus Meals! (*In a kind voice*) You can ladle me out a bowl
  of that piping-hot soup that you've just made!
Meals A pleasure, sir.

They both smile

Would sir like to eat a large selection of cakes as well?
Inspector (*quickly turning; unfriendly*) Shut up, Mrs Meals.

Bonecrusher enters, looking obviously mad

(*Heading for the exit*) Hallo, Boney! Come to steal some cakes?
Bonecrusher I like cooking. I like it a lot. (*He looks madly at Meals*) I had a pizza, once.
Meals That's good. You can give me a hand. You can start by crushing up some garlic. (*Pause*) Why are you lookin' at me like that, sir?

Bonecrusher puts his hands on Meals' skull

No I said the *garlic*, Mr Bonecraaaaaasaaaa!

The Lights cross-fade from R *to* L

The Inspector and Shutters (who must be played by the Darling actor at this point) enter the L *area, laughing uproariously*

Meals' scream gives way to the Inspector's laugh

Inspector Yes, yes — a fine joke, Shutters, a fine joke, but remember we have a serious matter on our hands. I want you to send in Tom Darling, straight away.
Shutters (*worriedly*) Straight away?
Inspector Yes, Shutters — straight away. Is there some sort of problem?
Shutters (*looking at his own costume*) No, sir.
Inspector Well then, man?

Shutters walks off removing his costume in full view of the audience, swearing under his breath

The Lights come up slowly R. *There is a commotion off-stage*

Darling enters, still dressing; with him is Scribbles, who is helping him, pointing out the fact that he is still wearing Shutters' wig

Inspector Mr Darling, Mrs Meals mentioned your alcoholic sister. If she's up, I should like to ask the broken-down drunk a few questions.
Darling (*in actor's own voice*) Is that all you got me in for?
Inspector (*in his own voice, but whispering*) OK, calm down.
Darling (*as above*) Do you realize how long it takes to change costume? It's hell back there!

The actors ad-lib an argument on stage. Scribbles reminds the actor playing Darling that there is an audience. For a second he is like a startled rabbit caught in headlights

Darling (*stiltedly*) Ah, Laura, send for Miss Daguerreotype.
Scribbles Right away, sir.

Scribbles pulls the wig off Darling's head and exits with it

Darling (*very seriously*) I must warn you, Inspector, my sister has a manly stride and a modern manner. You will find her somewhat, should I say — unconventional. The blackest of sheep. I would even go as for as to say that she's ——
Inspector (*worriedly*) Yes?
Darling (*gravely*) New-fangled.
Inspector (*more gravely*) Bloody hell!

Susan Daguerreotype enters. She is thirty-five-ish, attractive, and carries a real bottle

Susan (*to Darling*) I heard about Mary. (*Sarcastically*) What a shaaaaame! (*To Inspector*) Bloody hell — you're damned ug ——
Inspector (*cutting her off*) I know, you don't have to tell me, I'm damned ugly. Straight away, I see that you have a breezy, flip personality.

Susan Drunkenness is a major part of my character.

Inspector (*taking notes*) I see. Now, where were you this afternoon?

Darling She's been in bed all day with that headache.

Inspector (*flicking through the notebook*) Now, let me see — is that *Michael* Headache, the invisible professor? Now, it may be none of my business, Mr Darling, but this sounds very immoral.

Susan Yes, you're right — it *is* none of your business!

Inspector (*to Susan*) Excuse me, but since when were you called "Darling"?

Susan Ever since my blouses became too tight, Inspector.

The Inspector coughs and turns away, embarrassed

(*Heading for the exit*) Why, Inspector, your face has turned a rich shade of scarlet!

Susan exits

Inspector That's because you've given me a — beamer.

Darling (*looking at his feet*) Shan't stay around and, ah, aggravate the — the — beamer, old boy.

Darling shuffles off sheepishly

Shutters enters carrying his wig (real) and a note (real)

Shutters (*handing the note to the Inspector*) I'm afraid there's been another murder. This time it's Gentle John, the stableman. The note was left in one of his wellingtons.

Inspector (*reading*) "Yeast, yeast, yeast, yeast,
                          Johnny's head is rather creased."
Mmm, fine poem. Yeast. Shutters, will you send in Mrs Meals, the cook.

Shutters (*putting on the wig*) I'm afraid that will be impossible, sir. You see — she's dead.

The Inspector laughs

(*Producing a real mirror and checking the wig in it*) I got to her just as she was speaking her last words.

Inspector (*amused*) What did she say, Shutters?

Shutters Well, she asked *me* — —

Pause

Inspector (*grinning*) Yes?

Shutters — to ask you ——

Pause

Inspector (*grinning*) Yes?

Shutters If you would like to eat a large selection of cakes, sir.

Inspector (*suddenly serious*) And what did *I* say?

Shutters You said "Drop dead, Mrs Meals". (*Pause*) And she did.

Inspector So *I* killed her?

Shutters It certainly *looks* that way, sir.

Inspector My God. (*He is suddenly curious*) Where did you find her, Shutters?

Shutters In my wardrobe, sir.

Inspector In your wardrobe, Shutters?

Shutters In my wardrobe, sir.

Inspector In your wardrobe, Shutters?

Shutters In my wardrobe, sir.

Inspector In your wardrobe, Shutters?

Shutters In my wardrobe, sir.

There is a long pause

Inspector In your wardrobe, Shutters?

Shutters (*miming*) Yes, sir, I opened the wardrobe door and ——

Inspector (*cutting in*) Yes, yes, I know, the body fell out. This is commonpla ——

Shutters (*calmly*) No, Inspector.

Inspector No?

Shutters I took out a pair of boots and closed the door. I put the boots on and made to leave. Catching my reflection in the mirror, I noticed I had two *odd* boots on, so I went back, opened the wardrobe, and *then* the body fell out.

Inspector (*uncertainly*) I see.

Shutters She had this note attached to her body.

Shutters hands the real note to the Inspector

Inspector Thank you, Shutters. (*He reads the note*) "Roses are red, (*he pauses slightly*) The cook is dead". Another damned good piece of verse! Mmm, roses. Shutters, take me to the gardener.

Shutters The gardener, sir?

Inspector Yes, Shutters — the gardener.

Shutters The gardener, sir?

Inspector Yes, Shutters — the gardener.

Shutters The gard ——

Inspector (*shouting*) Shut up, Shutters, and just take me to the *bloody* gardener!

Shutters This way, sir.

The Inspector and Shutters exit

Black-out

Jeanie Skakles, the gardener, enters L

Two seconds later the Lights come up R. There are bird sounds

Shutters and the Inspector enter R

Shutters The gardener, sir. In the shed.

The Lights cross-fade from R to L

The set, stage L, is, nominally, a tiny shed. Jeanie Skakles is potting imaginary plants

The Inspector moves L, as if entering the shed. He immediately knocks imaginary things over. There are crashing sounds — made off stage. He apologises and bends down to pick things up, knocking down more in the process. Skakles looks on, unamused

Inspector Now, listen, I'm Detective Story — Scotland Yard. And your name is?

Skakles And my name is *what*?

Inspector That's what I'm asking — what is it?

Skakles Oh! Jeanie Skakles, Sir.

Inspector (*writing*) Skak — could you spell that?

Skakles No, sir.

Inspector (*slightly embarrassed*) Oh, never mind, you're probably quite good at weeding the garden.

Skakles No, sir.

Inspector (*floundering*) Well, then — you're probably a very nice person.

Skakles No, sir. And now, if you'd excuse me, I've work to dae for Mr Darling.

There is an almighty crash

Inspector Sorry. Concerning Mr Darling, Jeanie — what do you know about him?

Skakles Well, he's the master of the house, isn't he? He sells words for a livin', doesn't he?

Inspector (*to the audience*) Such a charming naiveté.

Skakles Eh?

Inspector One last question, noble gardener: did you hear any strange sounds this afternoon?

Skakles Well, now that you mention it, at five o'clock, when I was on the compost heap, I *did* hear somethin' rather preculiar.

The Inspector looks at the audience

Strange footsteps, wi' naeb'dy makin' them.

Inspector (*to the audience*) Such as might be made by an *invisible* man. (*To Skakles*) How did you know what time it was — you don't wear a watch. I would be surprised if you could even *tell* the time!

Skakles Oh, I knew for certain it was five. That's when I always go — regular as clockwork.

Inspector (*to the audience*) Can you believe this? (*He makes to leave*) Excuse me — I've got to go. Innuendo I *like*. But this is too ... (*He leaves the sentence unfinished. To the audience*) I'm sorry about this, everyone. (*He leaves the shed and heads* R)

Skakles Oh, are you? The only thing *you* should apologize about is your face, pal!

Bonecrusher, mad, enters R *and moves towards the shed, his arms outstretched*

Inspector (*pointing a finger at Skakles*) I hope you're next, Skakles. I *really* hope you're next!

Skakles sticks out her tongue. The Inspector returns the gesture

Inspector (*heading for the* R *exit*) Now, how *does* one find an invisible professor? (*He bumps into Bonecrusher*) Oh, hallo, Bonecrusher.

The Inspector moves into the darkness R

Bonecrusher (*walking toward Skakles, mad*) I like flowers. I like them a lot. They're very delicate.

Skakles Well, growing flowers takes a lot of skill, stranger. Can you crush up some of that horse dung? It makes a *great* fertilizer.

Bonecrusher enters the shed. There are crashing noises. He reaches for Skakles' head

Skakles No, I said *the horse dung,* sir — it's really not that hard to tell us apaaaaaaaaaart!

The Lights cross-fade from L *to* R

We are now, nominally, back in the drawing-room

The Inspector sneezes, the sound merging into that of Skakles' cry

Inspector Aaaaaaaa-choo! Mmm, cold coming on.

During the following, the Lights gradually come up L

(*Pacing up and down*) Right, I must say, this is the first time in my career that I've interviewed someone I couldn't see, Professor, but I'll carry on regardless.

Professor (*voice-over*) Make it quick — I'm a busy man.

Inspector (*still pacing*) Now, I'm sure you'll have heard about the recent mad multiple murders?

Professor (*voice-over; from the other side of the room*) Terrible business. Me? I'm the cheery type. (*He sings a snippet of a current chart hit*)

Inspector (*searching for the Professor*) And you'll also realize that you have a natural advantage over everyone else. You could kill without being noticed. No-one knows where you are at any given time. You could easily — (*he knocks heads with the Professor*) — OW! Now, *that* illustrates my point perfectly. (*He walks away, looking at where the voice has just come from*) Will you be kind enough to tell me where you were this afternoon?

Professor I was on the four-twenty train from London.

Inspector (*turning quickly around and colliding with the Professor*) Oww! I don't believe you! I sense much ruthlessness festering behind that charming little goatee beard.

There is the sound of someone being hit; the Inspector reacts as if he has been hit

Oww! I see my senses don't deceive me.

Another sound effect; again he reacts as if hit

Oww! So *that's* your game, is it? (*He takes his coat off and rolls up his shirt sleeves*) Put your dukes up! Take *that!* (*He "hits" the Professor*)

There is the sound of a clap from off stage

And that! (*He "hits" the Professor again*)

Clap!

Pause

(*Proud of his boxing*) Had enough, have you?

Pause. The Inspector reacts as if he has been kneed between the legs by the Invisible Man and then punched in the face

OK, Professor, the kid gloves are off!

There follows a wrestling match with all the classic clinches, e.g. banging the canvas floor, half nelsons, chinese burns etc. The Inspector bends the Professor's limbs in impossible ways. We end on the Professor's head being twisted around three times between the Inspector's legs

Inspector A one-a! A two-a! A three-a! YOU'RE OUT!

Susan enters. She looks at the Inspector, puzzled

Susan Inspector, you're a nutter.
Inspector I've just been wrestling — with the invisible professor.
Susan (*looking the Inspector up and down*) I'm very pleased for you.
Inspector (*looking around*) Yes. I won.
Susan Inspector, the man's ninety-seven years old. Of course you won. (*She moves to the phonograph and picks a record off the turntable. She looks at the label*) Oh ... Jeanie, the gardener — she was found on the compost heap.
Inspector (*smiling. To the audience*) Gosh! I say — that's blasted unfortunate.
Susan (*putting the record on*) Why, I'm beginning to like you, Inspector.

Tango music begins to play

Susan grabs the Inspector

Let's tango.
Inspector But I don't know how ——
Susan Shut up and dance.

During the following, Susan and the Inspector execute a ridiculously complex tango, the Inspector taking the woman's part

Inspector You're so strong. I love a woman who leads.
Susan You're nice.
Inspector You're beautiful.
Susan I know. And I'll tell you *this* for nothing: it may not seem obvious to you, but *I* never killed *anyone* — as sure as my name's Susan Daguerreotype.
Inspector (*suddenly fierce*) But *is* your name Susan Daguerreotype? In Germany in 1912, a mad doctor/scientist searching for the secret of life, fell into a seamy half-world ——
Susan Very interesting, I'm sure Inspector — but I fail to see what it has to do with the case.
Inspector Do you, Mrs Daguerreotype? Or should I say "Herr Schwitters"? For you are a mad, struck-off doctor! Et cetera, et cetera, et cetera.

The music stops suddenly

Susan I admit it, but I still didn't kill anyone.
Inspector Then who did?

There is a clap of thunder and a flash of lightning

Black-out

Susan exits

The Lights come up

*Darling and Tom Jnr enter. Tom Jnr carries an imaginary toy gun
and wears a cap*

Tom Jnr Will I see Mama in heaven, papa?

Darling Of course, young Tommy. Of course. Now, the nice
Inspector wants a *nice* little chat with you, young Tommy; is that
all right?

Tom Jnr Of course, Papa.

Inspector (*adopting the voice which adults often use to speak to
children*) Hallo there, young Tommy. And what did we do at
school today?

Tom Jnr (*playing with the gun, not looking at the Inspector*) You
weren't there, stupid! And if you were, you wouldn't have to ask,
would you? (*He looks at the Inspector*) Papa! He looks like he was
born inside-out!

Inspector (*tossing a real coin*) Oh, look, young Tommy: half-a-
crown!

Tom Jnr (*imitating the Inspector's voice*) "Oh, look, young
Tommy: half-a-crown".

Inspector (*friendly*) Don't you want it?

Tom Jnr "Don't you want it?"

Inspector (*staying calm and friendly*) Now, listen, Tommy ——

Tom Jnr "Now, listen, Tommy ——"

Inspector (*loudly*) I'D LIKE TO ASK YOU A FEW QUESTIONS!

Pause

Tom Jnr Can you whistle? *I* can whistle!

Inspector Why yes, I can, young Tommy. (*He whistles*)

Tom Jnr (*in the Inspector's face*) I've got a gun. BANG! BANG!
BANG!

Inspector That's a *splendid* gun you have there, young fellow!

Tom Jnr Bang! Bang!

Inspector Now. Tommy. Did you hear anything odd this
after ——

Tom Jnr Bang! Bang!

Inspector (*smiling, trying to hold in his anger*) Yes, Tommy —
I've already said — it's a splendid gun. Now ——

Tom Jnr Bang! Bang! Bang!

Inspector (*losing patience*) Now look, Tommy — it's not *that* splendid!

Tom Jnr Bang! Bang! Bang! Bang! Bang! Bang! Bang!

The Inspector looks at the audience; after the fifth of the following "Bangs" he punches Tom Jnr in the stomach

Bang! Bang! Bang! Bang! Bang! Ba ——

Inspector BANG!

Tommy falls crumpled to the floor

Darling (*stepping over Tommy*) Inspector!

Inspector I never *touched* him!

Tommy crawls off

Darling You're *really* big, aren't you? Really big. How would you like it if some big brute manhandled *you*? Beating and humiliating you? How would you like *that,* Inspector?

Inspector Very much! Yes, *very* much. (*He pauses*) Cost a pretty packet, thought. Straight sex is pretty cheap these days, but to get something a bit, you know — *special*, you really have to shell out — don't you find?

Darling I ... I can't believe what you're saying!

Inspector Oh, yes — 'strue: I remember when you could get yourself trussed up and beaten for ten shillings; now it's a least a guinea and these modern skinny tarts have no muscle. No stamina.

Darling (*shocked*) Oh!

Inspector You share my revulsion. Yes, give me a powerfully built woman with a bit of severity any day. I meant to ask, did you ever, you know ... Mrs Meals ... ?

Darling Why, you filthy ——

Inspector (*full of admiration*) You did, didn't you! You *lucky* beggar!

Scribbles enters

Scribbles Oh, excuse me, sir, did Young Danny Travis used to be
alive?
Darling Pardon, Laura?
Scribbles Young Danny Travis, sir. He hasn't *always* been dead,
has he?
Darling What?
Scribbles It's just that I found his body in the conservatory when
I was in the hall dusting the library.
Darling Inspector! We're *all* going to die!
Inspector (*stepping forward; calmly and slowly*) Now, Laura, just
prior to finding him, did you hear any screams and if you did, at
exactly what time did you hear them?
Scribbles It was eleven twenty-seven, sir, *exactly* — but I didn't
hear no screams.
Inspector You didn't?
Scribbles Yes.
Inspector Is that yes, you *did* hear screams, or yes, you didn't?
Scribbles That's yes I ain't, but did never didn't not hear none, ever,
sir.
Inspector That doesn't make any sense.
Scribbles I'm a surrealist, beggin' your pardon, sir.
Inspector (*to the audience*) I think I'll join in on this crazy banter.

*The Inspector and Scribbles both take a step forward, lit only by the
footlights, and continue as if they were a hackneyed music hall act*

Inspector So, you didn't hear these screams at exactly eleven
twenty-seven. At what time was that, roughly?
Scribbles It might have been eleven twenty-seven, sir — I'm not
sure.
Inspector Well, what were you doing at eleven twenty-seven?
Scribbles I was looking at my watch.
Inspector What time was it then?
Scribbles I can't recall, sir. (*Helpfully*) It might have been half-past
six.

Inspector And what were you doing at half past ——
Darling Inspector! Young Danny's dead, and you are just questioning Laura for the sheer blasted fun of it!

The Lights revert to their previous state

Inspector Guilty.
Scribbles If I get killed can I have the day off, sir?
Darling (*flatly*) Laura, you're fired.
Scribbles (*heading for the exit, relieved*) Oh, thank you, sir!

Scribbles exits

Inspector Now, one of you is a killer. Just who, I don't know. Yet. But one of you: Darling, Daguerreotype, Uncle, Shutters, Scribbles, Bonecrusher is a killer. (*He raises hand*) And I *know* what you're going to say — but names can be misleading. You should not always look for the obvious. My last case, for example: the suspects included Alister Madman, James Death and Lawrence Evil, but a chap named Peter Innocent turned out to be the actual murderer. But this case is simple. Very simple. In fact, it's a bit *too* simple for my liking. In fact, it's so simple that — that I can't work it out. (*Pause*) It's a *hard* case. A *very* hard case. A bit *too* hard for my liking. I like the easy ones best. I can *do* them. It's the hard ones I'm not so keen on. Easy ones — no problem; hard ones ... ? (*He gesticulates and draws a sharp breath suggesting difficulty*) Woooooa. (*Quickly*) Of course we could just blame it on the little boy, no?
Darling That's *it*, Inspector! You've been wasting our time with jokes of a rather disgusting nature, while we all stand around like idiots — waiting to get killed.
Inspector I still think *you're* doing this, Darling!
Darling But listen, man! You were with me when my wife was killed!
Inspector I only have your word for that, Mr Darling. I read one of your books, once: a high-pitched suspenseful thriller whose blood-curdling narrative kept me *leashed* to my armchair! It was

set in an asylum, Mr Darling. Frightening, yes. But I never thought the author capable of murder of a three-dimensional nature. That is, until today.

Uncle enters

Uncle Tom!

Darling Surely you're not suggesting I ——

Inspector The title of that book was ... Well, why don't *you* tell us, Mr Darling?

Darling I've written over eight hundred novels — I can't be expected to remember them all!

Inspector Then let me refresh your memory. It was called *The Bonecrusher*.

Darling reacts with shock and surprise

Remember it *now*, Darling?

Darling (*quietly*) Yes, it seems to ring a bell.

Inspector Pardon, Mr Darling, we didn't quite catch that?

Darling I've got a new novel to write. I'm going to the library. I don't want to be disturbed.

Inspector Then don't think of all the gruesome murders you've committed.

Uncle You've the *devil* in you, Tom Darling! I've always thought that! I should never have allowed you to marry Mary!

Darling Uncle, can't you see what he's doing? He's setting us all against each other. How do we know he's even a real detective?

Uncle What do you mean. You think he might just be pretending? He might, just be kidding on? Just joshing us, like? Spinning us a yarn? Mmmm, if he is, he's quite good at it, Tom.

Darling Need I remind you, Inspector, that the murders began when *you* arrived?

Uncle Yes, just who are you, Inspector? Where did you come from?

Inspector I told you: my car is stuck in a ditch half a ——

Darling You don't really expect us to believe that do you, Inspector? I had Shutters go down the road to see. There is no such car in any of the many ditches that surround this house. I don't even think you've got a car, Inspector. And do you know what? I don't even think you're in the police force. You've probably never been in a ditch in your life! I bet you don't even know what a ditch is! (*He stands face-to-face with the Inspector*) I don't like you, Inspector. I don't like *you one bit*! *I* don't like your manner and I don't like your mind. I don't even like your shoes. (*Pause*) I don't like your *shirt*; I don't like your *tie* and I *don't* like your jacket. (*He looks away, embarrassed*) I've pretended all along that I don't like your moustache, but I must admit, it's quite good. (*He turns back to face the Inspector. Loudly*) But I *don't* like your face, I *don't* like your hair and I *don't* like the way you walk! (*He looks away, speaking quietly*) I quite like your pipe.

Pause

Inspector I quite like *your* pipe.

Pause

Darling You do?
Inspector Of *course* I do.
Darling Really?
Inspector Yes, really.
Darling You're not just saying that?
Inspector It's a de*lightful* pipe. It's a *beautiful pipe* — in fact, it's the most divine pipe I've seen in my whole life.

There is a pause. Darling and the Inspector move towards each other, pipes in mouths. The pipes touch. Pause. They make strange animalistic noises and put each other's pipes in each other's mouths

Susan enters holding Tom Jnr's cap

Susan Excuse me, Inspector — sorry to interrupt, but I found *this* in the hall.

Darling (*taking the cap*) Young Tommy! Is he all right?

Susan Well, put it this way: it doesn't fit any more.

Darling (*weeping into the cap*) TOMMY!!

Susan (*cruelly*) Awwwwwww!

Darling (*making to leave*) My life is not worth living! I'm going to *kill* myself!

Darling exits

Susan Inspector, for heaven's sake, hurry up and solve this case or there will be none of us left!

There is a gunshot off stage

Inspector Yes, you're right. (*Pause*) Right! Time to get to work! (*Pause*) Right! (*Pause*) Damn it, I've *still* no bloody idea who did it, you know. Mmm. Uncle, you don't *like* living things, do you? Your stuffed souvenir tiger and elephant heads which adorn almost every inch of these walls are *ample* evidence of that fact. You aren't satisfied until something is stuffed and mounted, are you?

Uncle If this is some kind of joke, I find it in extremely poor taste! You are a very impudent young man, Inspector. I may be fiendishly bad tempered, but I *didn't kill* all those *people*.

Inspector Soon you'll be in prison — far from the muffin-festooned fireside of Farmbright Mansion!

Uncle Fiddlesticks!

Inspector You killed the handyman, Uncle!

Uncle Bosh!

Inspector And then you killed Mrs Darling!

Uncle Balderdash!

Inspector You then you killed, eh, the next person who was killed!

Uncle Humbug!

Inspector And then you killed the person after that!

Uncle Tommy rot!

Inspector You killed them all, Uncle!

Uncle Shite! I mean, "fudge"! Fudge and, ah ——

Susan Gobbledegook, Uncle?

Uncle Yes. Fudge and pure and utter gobbledegook! Thank you, Susan.

Inspector OK then, Uncle, what *were* you doing at the time of the first murder?

Uncle I was out jogging. I mean I was ——

Inspector *Just* as I thought.

Susan (*shocked*) Uncle!! Why pretend for forty years that you couldn't walk?

Uncle I couldn't think of anything *else* to do with my life! But I didn't kill Mary! Nor the rest!

Inspector Didn't you, Uncle? Or should I say "Aunty', for that moustache is fooling no-one! (*He pulls off Uncle's moustache*)

Susan gasps

Uncle (*standing up, letting the tartan rug fall, revealing a skirt*) OK, I admit it — I'm a woman. But I am an *innocent* woman. My real name is Miss Bunty McPherson. My hobbies are needlepoint and cake eating. (*She heads for the exit*) Does anyone want anything at the shop?

Uncle exits

Susan No thanks, Bunty.

Susan } (*together*) Strange woman!
Inspector

Inspector But as harmless as a common household fly.

Shutters enters carrying an imaginary pair of legs

Shutters Excuse me, but I found these in the hall.

Susan It's the invisible professor's legs!

Inspector My God!

Shutters That's not all, sir: look behind you.

Inspector Why, it's the poor devil's torso! (*He picks the imaginary torso up*)

They join the legs and the torso together. Susan spots an imaginary arm, picks it up and returns to the others

Susan (*joining the arm to the torso*) Here's one of his arms.
Inspector (*picking up another arm and joining it to the torso*) And here's the other! My God! *No-one* deserves to die this way! Now, gently — *put* him down.

They put the professor down. Pause

I feel a prayer is in order here. (*He looks up to the heavens*)

The others follow suit. Pause

(*Looking at another part of the heavens*) Anyone know any?

No takers

No? How about some — apt words? Apt words, Susan? Shutters? No? (*Pause*) Jokes. Anyone got any good jokes — for this wretched man; this — this — just a minute! Where's the poor blighter's noggin?

They all look around, standing still

Bonecrusher enters, throwing and catching the imaginary head whilst making monster-like noises

Ah! Well found, Bonecrusher!

Bonecrusher throws the head up — but too high. They all follow its fall into the audience. Thud!

Don't worry Boney — I'll fetch it! (*He strolls into the audience whistling and picks up the head. He is about to rejoin the others when a thought strikes him*) Just a minute! It's suddenly dawned on me whodidit!

Dramatic music

It's been staring me in the blasted face all blinking night! (*He points to an audience member*) Here's your guilty man! My assistant and I have been watching you all evening, mister! You haven't laughed *once*!

Susan steps down into the audience, the others behind her

Susan During the excitement of the play, you've been sneaking off to the wings and killing us off one by one!

Bonecrusher You thought you were above suspicion!

Inspector You thought you'd get away with it, didn't you? *Didn't* you?

Shutters It's the prison for you!

Bonecrusher I had you earmarked from the start, Sonny Jim!

Inspector So, you think this is a big *joke* do you?

Susan Well, no, he doesn't — that's the whole point, surely.

Bonecrusher You damned bloody damned killer!

Shutters *You* dood it!

Bonecrusher Well done, Inspector: another case wrapped up.

The music stops. They all clap and cheer

Inspector Cuff the bastard, Boney.

Susan and Shutters take the Inspector back on to the stage, congratulating him. They are joined by Bonecrusher and the "murderer"

Susan One last thing, Inspector. You said you and your "assistant". Just who *is* this "assistant"?

Inspector Why, it's Sergeant Bonecrusher of the yard! Oh, what a *merry* ending!

Everyone laughs, starting and stopping simultaneously

One last thing! Susan — will you marry me?

Susan OK.
Shutters And will you marry me, Mr Bonecrusher?
Bonecrusher A pleasure, old sport!
Shutters A *double* wedding!!
All Hoorah! Hoorah! Hoorah!

Black-out

*Three seconds later, the lights come back up for the bows, with
music*

FURNITURE AND PROPERTY LIST

Off stage: Wheelchair and rug (**Uncle**)
Two pitchforks (**Stage Management**)

Personal: **Darling**: pipe
Uncle: glasses, bottle of "meths"
Inspector: pipe, notepad with pen attached, coin, handkerchief
Scribbles: duster, paper note
Shutters: wig, paper note, small vanity mirror
Meals: wooden spoon, paper note
Susan: gin bottle
Smart: helmet, truncheon

LIGHTING PLOT

Practical fittings required: nil
An empty stage. The same throughout

To open: Darkness

Cue 1	Music. Doorbell *Bring up general interior lights*	(Page 1)
Cue 2	Doorbell *Lightning flash*	(Page 3)
Cue 3	**Bonecrusher**: " — damned blasted mouth shut." *Lightning flash*	(Page 3)
Cue 4	Dramatic chords; after third chord *Flash of lightning*	(Page 8)
Cue 5	**Uncle** exits quickly *Flash of lightning*	(Page 11)
Cue 6	**Mrs Meals** enters *Flash of lightning*	(Page 12)
Cue 7	**Scribbles**: " …beggin' your pardon, sir." *Black-out*	(Page 15)
Cue 8	Thunderclap. Music *Bring up lights to previous setting*	(Page 15)
Cue 9	**Travis, the Inspector** and **Shutters** exit *Black out; two seconds pause; bring up interior lights* L	(Page 20)

Cue 10   **Stableman**: "NO! NO!" (He screams)   (Page 22)
            Cross-fade lights from L *to* R

Cue 11   **Meals**: " … Mr Bonecraaaaaasaaaa!"   (Page 24)
            Cross-fade lights from R *to* L

Cue 12   **Shutters** exits   (Page 24)
            Bring up lights slowly R

Cue 13   **The Inspector** and **Shutters** exit   (Page 28)
            Black-out

Cue 14   **Skakles** enters. Two seconds pause   (Page 28)
            Bring up lights R

Cue 15   **Skakles**: "—— tell us apaaaaaaaaart!"   (Page 30)
            Cross-fade lights from L *to* R

Cue 16   **The Inspector**: "Mmm, cold coming on."   (Page 31)
            Bring up lights gradually L

Cue 17   Thunder   (Page 33)
            Flash of lightning; black-out

Cue 18   **Susan** exits   (Page 33)
            Bring up general interior lights

Cue 19   **The Inspector** and **Scribbles** take a step forward   (Page 36)
            Black-out all lights except footlights

Cue 20   **Darling**: " … for the sheer blasted fun of it!"   (Page 37)
            Bring up general interior lights

Cue 21   **All**: "Hoorah! Hoorah! Hoorah!"   (Page 44)
            Blackout; three seconds pause, then bring up general lights

EFFECTS PLOT

Cue 12	Black-out *Thunderclap. Music*	(Page 15)
Cue 13	Lights come up *Music fades*	(Page 15)
Cue 14	**Darling**: "You're feeding yourself these lines!" *Sad violin music*	(Page 17)
Cue 15	**The Inspector** returns to normal *Music cut*	(Page 18)
Cue 16	**The Inspector**: " … in this nightmarish mansion." *Thunder*	(Page 18)
Cue 17	**Travis**: " … you hum it and I'll join in." *Burst of over-enthusiastic canned laughter and applause*	(Page 19)
Cue 18	**The Inspector** grabs **Travis** by the collar *Laughter and applause cut*	(Page 19)
Cue 19	**Bonecrusher**: "I like horses." *Horse neighs*	(Page 21)
Cue 20	**Bonecrusher**: "I like them a lot." *Horse neighs*	(Page 21)
Cue 21	**Stableman** screams *Whistling kettle*	(Page 22)
Cue 22	**Meals**: "Some tea, Inspector?" *Whistle sound fades*	(Page 22)
Cue 23	Lights come up R *Bird sounds*	(Page 28)
Cue 24	**The Inspector** knocks things over *Crashing sounds off stage*	(Page 29)
Cue 25	**Bonecrusher** enters the shed *Crashing noises*	(Page 30)

Cue 26   **The Inspector**: " ... charming little goatee beard." (Page 31)
            Sound of someone being hit

Cue 27   **The Inspector**: " ... my senses don't deceive me." (Page 31)
            Sound of someone being hit

Cue 28   **The Inspector** "hits" the **Professor**   (Page 31)
            Clap

Cue 29   **The Inspector** "hits" the **Professor** again   (Page 32)
            Clap off stage

Cue 30   **Susan**: "Why, I'm beginning to like you, Inspector."(Page 32)
            Tango music

Cue 31   **Inspector**: "Et cetera, et cetera, et cetera."   (Page 33)
            Music stops suddenly

Cue 32   **The Inspector**: "Then who did?"   (Page 33)
            Clap of thunder

Cue 33   **Susan**: " ... or there will be none of us left!"   (Page 40)
            Gunshot

Cue 34   **The Inspector**: " ... whodidit!"   (Page 42)
            Dramatic music

Cue 35   **Bonecrusher**: " ... another case wrapped up."   (Page 43)
            Music stops

Cue 36   Bring up lights for bows   (Page 44)
            Music

Lightning Source UK Ltd.
Milton Keynes UK
UKOW06f1112210416

272687UK00012B/194/P